FRENCH CUISINE

A Frog's Guide

ALICE OEHR

ALBERT VERTE GRENOUILLE
Executive chef, Bistro Grenouille, Paris

Bienvenue

Welcome to France. A country of fabulous art, beautiful women, timeless architecture and sexy accents. Visitors come for the Eiffel Tower, the Notre-Dame, the Monalisa ... then they embark on the *real* pleasures of France – at the table. It is to these that we frogs are most dedicated.

Crusty bread, flaky pastries, lusciously rich and delicate cakes. French Champagne – the real Champagne – and wines in red, white and *rosé* colours. We make hundreds of varieties of creamy, smelly cheese from every four-legged animal you've ever seen on a farm. We braise those same animals in classic casseroles or simply sauté and serve them with one of our famous French sauces. Elegant and exquisite is our cuisine, drawing upon centuries of tradition. I invite you to enjoy it in the pages that follow.

Thousands of my amphibious brothers have donated their legs to the kitchen and I shall, one day, willingly give mine.

AVG

– Albert V. Grenouille

Menu

Boulangerie & Patisserie

Baguette – Brioche – Croissant – Pain au Chocolat
Escargot – Tarte au Citron – Millefeuille
Èclair – Madeleine – Macaron – Canelé

Gourmandises & Fromages

Truffe – Terrine – Foie Gras – Saussisson – Escargots
Cuisses de Grenouille –Crudités – Tapenade
Roquefort – Camembert – Fromage du Chèvre – Comté

Déjeuner

Croque Monsieur – Croque Madame – Quiche Lorraine
Soupe a l'Oignon – Salade Niçoise – Pissaladière

Plats

Steak Frîtes – Tartare de Bœuf – Coq au Vin
Cassoulet – Choucroute Garnie – Bouillabaisse
Bœuf Bourguignon – Confit de Canard

Desserts

Mont Blanc – Île Flottante – Profiteroles – Crêpes
Soufflé – Pêche Melba – Mousse au Chocolat
Tarte Tatin – Crème Caramel – Crème Brûlée

Boissons

Café au Lait – Cognac – Pastis
Kir Royale – Vin – Champagne

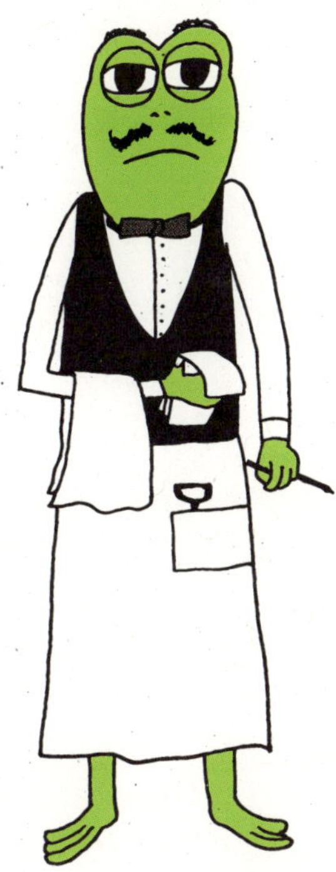

Boulangerie & Patisserie

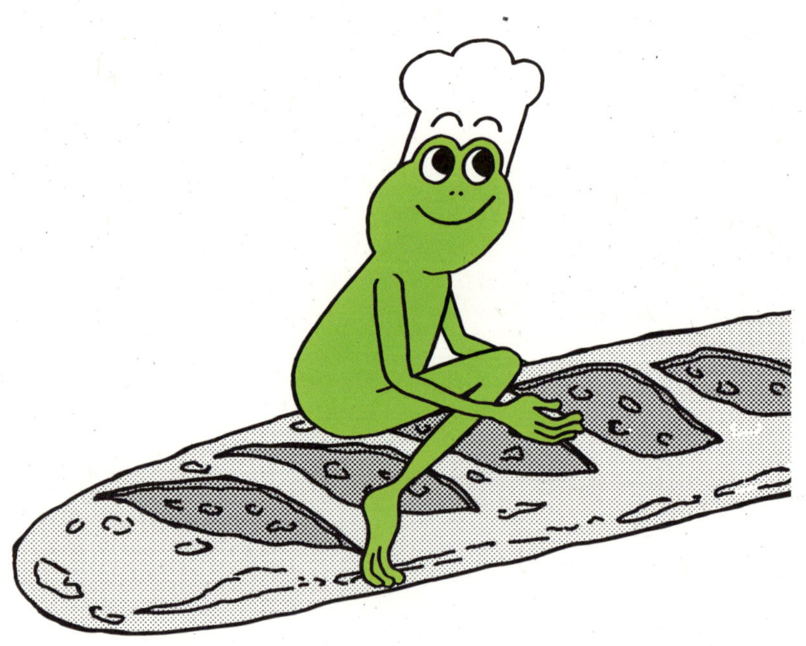

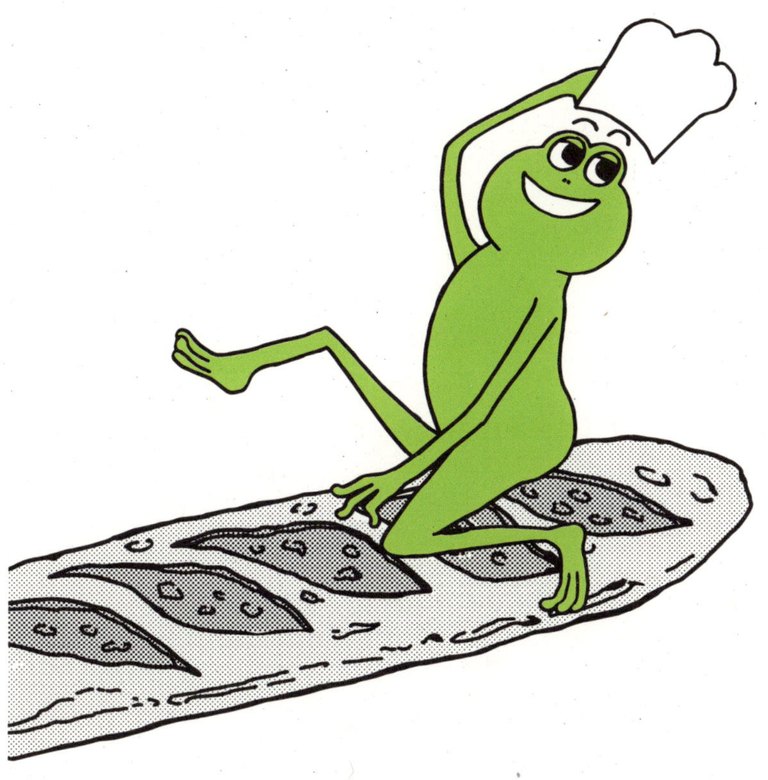

Baguette

The inimitable golden baton of the *boulangerie*, served at the side of every meal. Must be fermented overnight under a special blanket. Must be kept warm during transportation under the armpit (small nibbles off the end are permissible). Must never be sliced with a knife, only broken with fingers. Must be employed like a sponge at the end of a meal to save on the washing up.

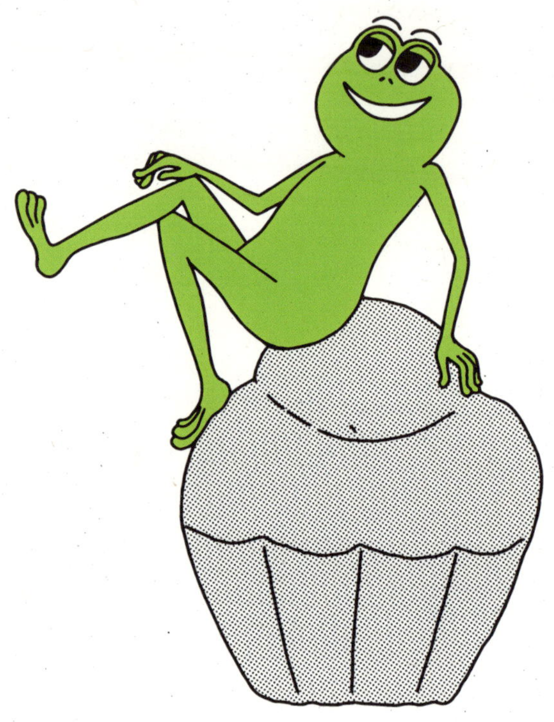

Brioche

Golden proof that bread is better with the addition of butter and eggs. The classic *brioche-tête* has a little head on top of its plump cake shape. Additions to the original may include orange blossom water, chocolate chips or raisins. For die-hard fans, a loaf form is available.

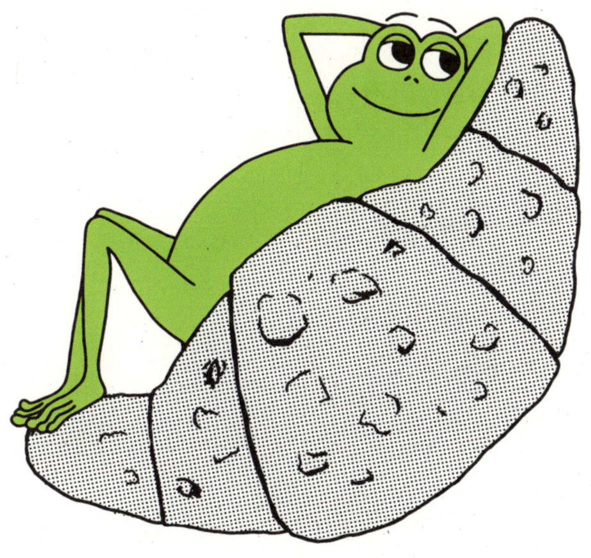

Croissant

The crescent-shaped start to a Frenchman's morning – pure butter only *s'il vous plait*. This, the most iconic output of the French *pâtisserie*, requires only two things for it's creation: butter – many kilograms, and a baker's biceps – many hours. Should you happen to gaze skyward on a starry night, you may observe this pastry.

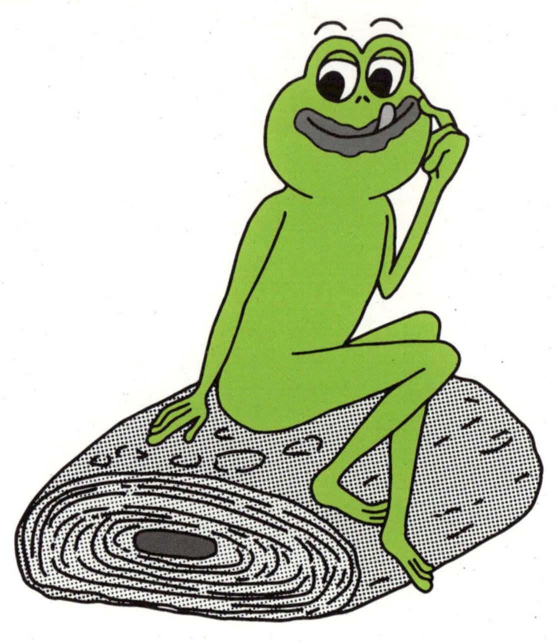

Pain au Chocolat

The only thing nicer than a warm, flaky *croissant* fresh from the oven is the very same thing with a thick bar of chocolate nestled inside – two bars, if you're lucky. Call this pastry a *Chocolatine* to sound like a local. Acceptable fare for breakfast or an afternoon pick-me-up.

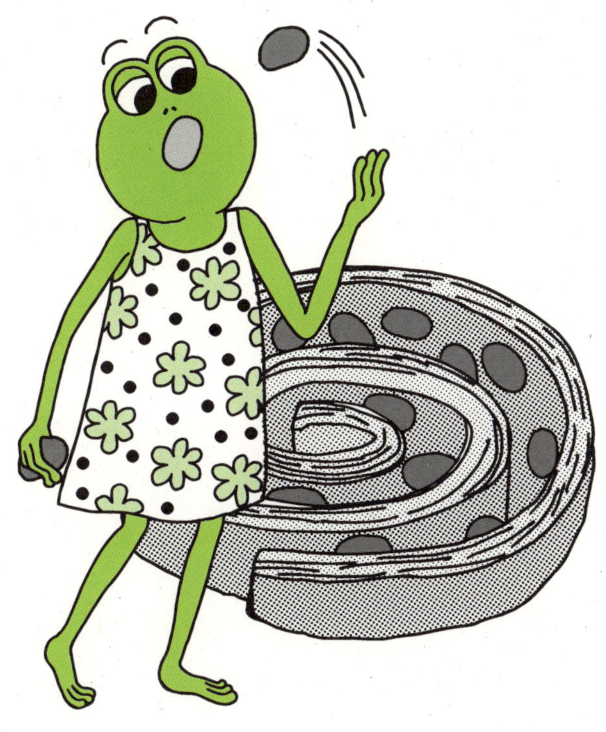

Escargot

A snail-inspired spiral of puff pastry wrapped around a few raisins and a good slathering of *crème pâtissière*. Despite its name, no molluscs are involved in the making of this pastry.

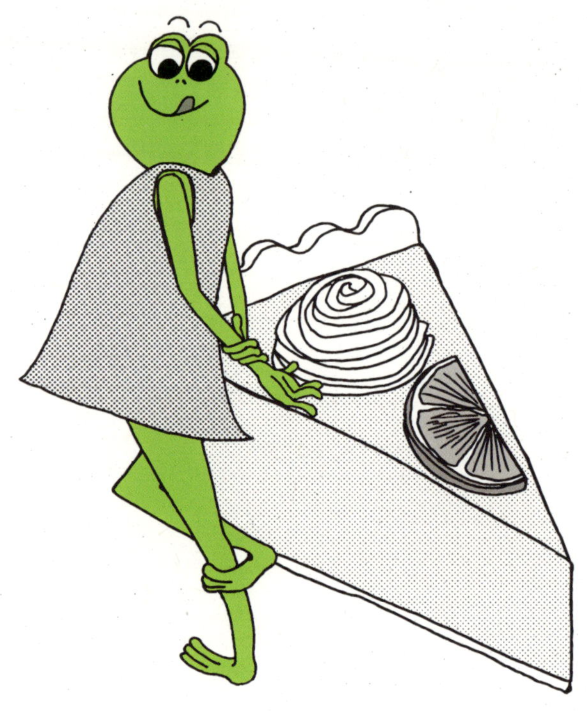

Tarte au Citron

A citrussy celebration of the great romance between sweet and sour. The lemon curd filling may wear a decorative *chapeau* of toasted *meringue* in some *pâtisseries*. Like French women, the pastry case must be enviably thin and delicate.

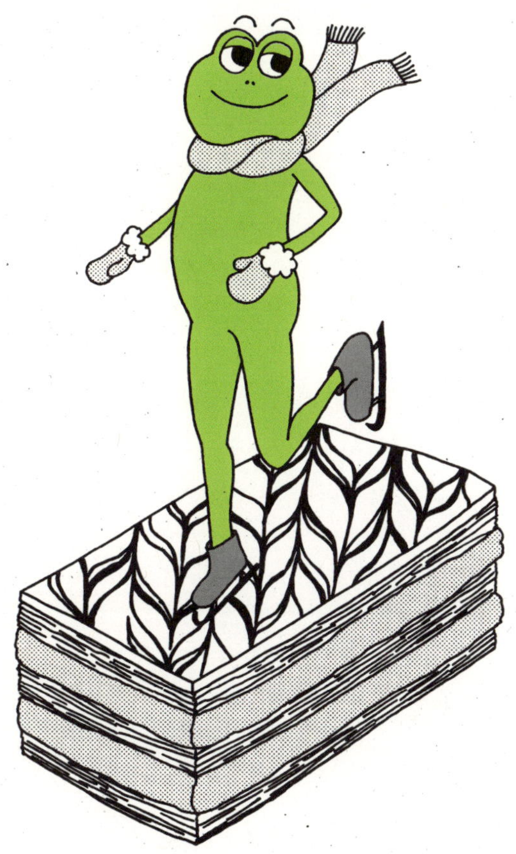

Millefeuille

An elegant, double-storey vanilla slice with a signature marbled fondant top. Three levels of flaky pastry are seasoned with the sweat of the poor *pâtissiers* who roll them out some 1000 times. Lusciously thick pastry cream provides additional fortification to the structure. Don't bother sharing, it's completely un-sliceable.

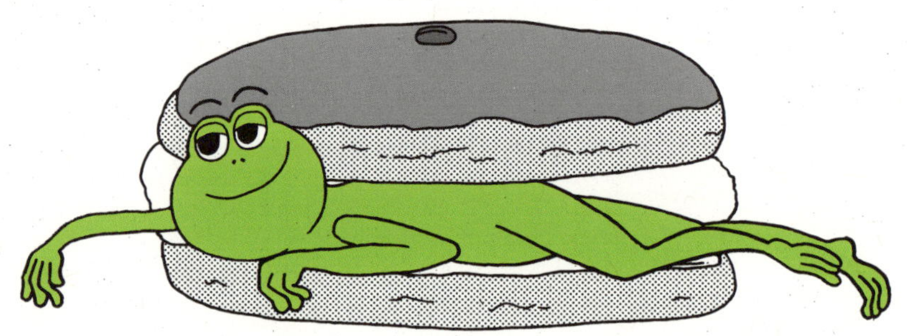

Èclair

An iced, cream-filled baton that goes down as quick as lightning, for which it was named. Flavours include coffee, chocolate, pistachio or *crème Chantilly* with hard toffee on top. None of the above will remotely hinder the speed of consumption.

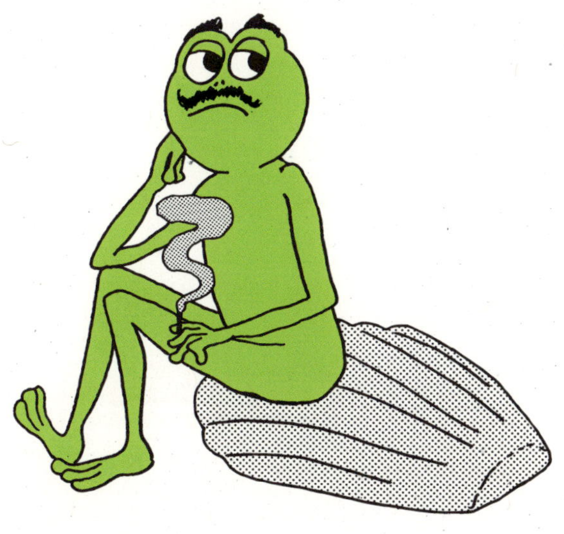

Madeleine

While *beurre noisette* and lemon zest give these cakes their flavour, it's the note of *nostalgie* on the palette – specifically for one's childhood – that really lingers. Fashioned in the pretty form of a scallop shell, the *Madeleine* has acquired fans around the globe – and not just pensive young writers moping in their rooms.

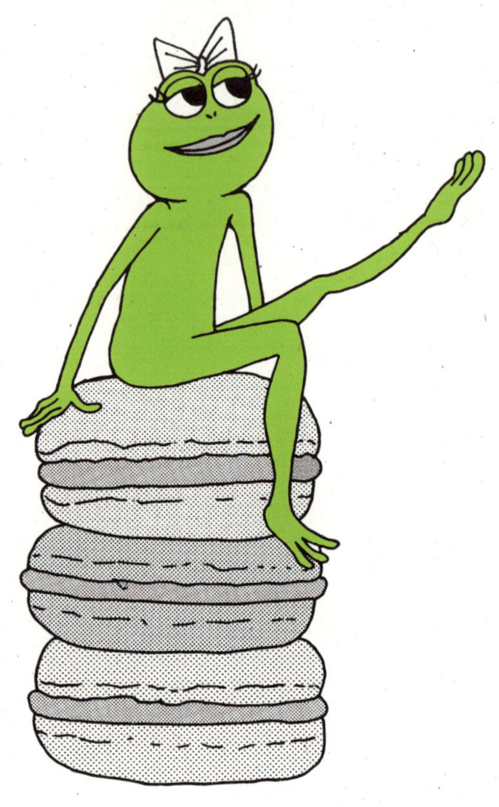

Macaron

The candy-coloured darlings *du moment* of the French *pâtisserie*. Each *macaron* is comprised of two fluffy almond *meringues* sandwiched together with *gânache*. Flavourings should be simple and elegant – coffee, lemon, pistachio, lavender, raspberry – but look out for their *gauche* cousins in Bubblegum and Piña Colada, often seen stacked in towers at girly parties.

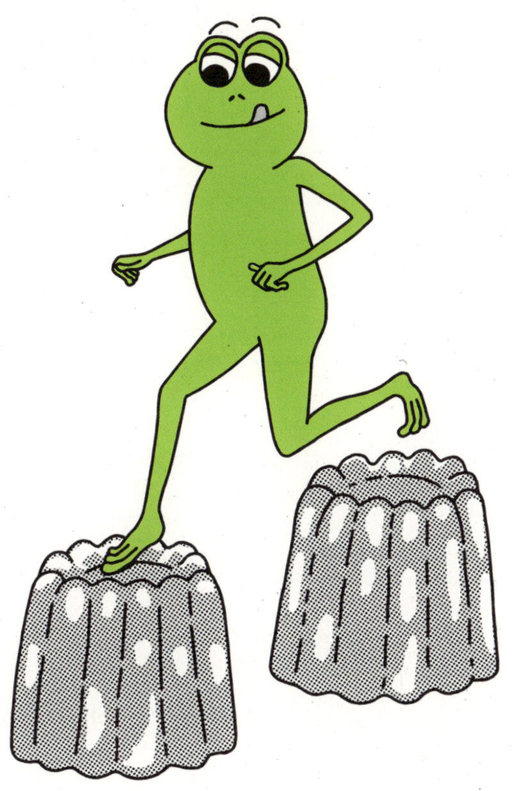

Canelé

A basic batter rendered elegant by the fluted shape of the copper mould in which it's baked. Flavoured delicately with *rhum* and *vanille*, *canelés* are embalmed in beeswax and baked until crunchy on the outside and delightfully chewy within. They come from Bordeaux in neat little sets of 8 or 16.

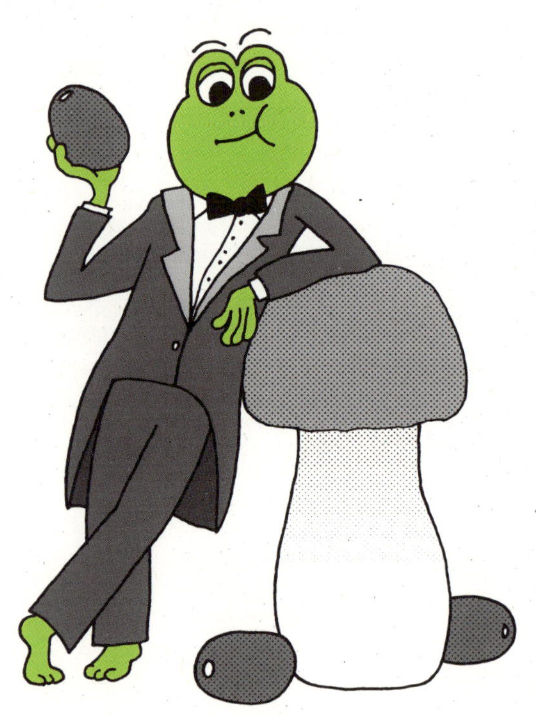

Gourmandises & Fromages

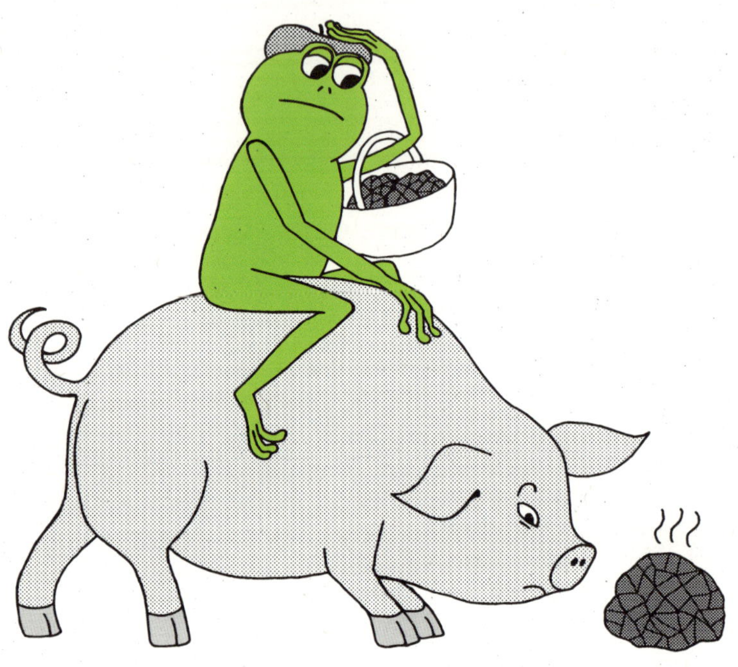

Truffe

A beloved delicacy of the pig, hijacked *en route* from ground to snout by a greedy truffle hunter, who distracts the animal with a slice of *saucisson* (a little cannibalistic, but effective nonetheless). Though they occasionally lose a finger to the pigs, professional trufflers are rewarded generously in this high-stress game with astronomical returns on their goods. Serve sparingly, in wafer-thin slivers atop eggs, pasta or *foie gras*.

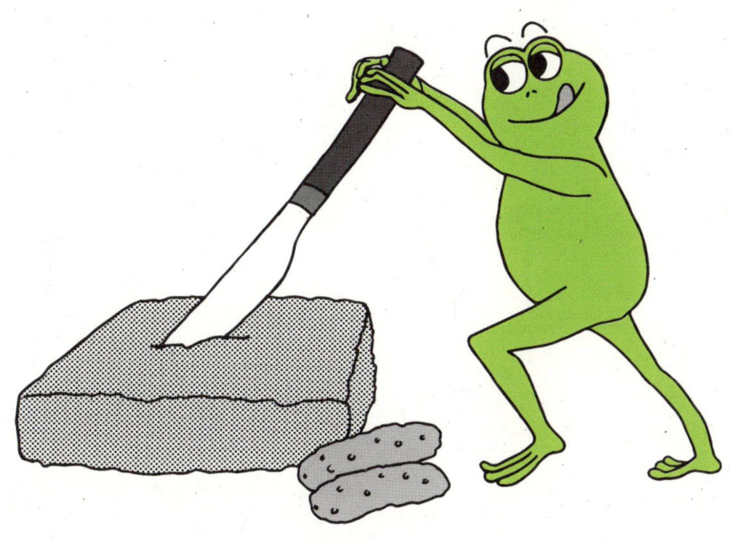

Terrine

A slab of ground meat – pig, cow, duck, quail, pheasant, wild boar, rabbit – flavoured with herbs, lard and wine. May be baked *en croûte* (in pastry) or enrobed in bacon for variety. Serve cold, with *baguette* and mini pickled *cornichons*. A close relative, *pâté*, is (usually) made purely from livers for a little extra cholesterol.

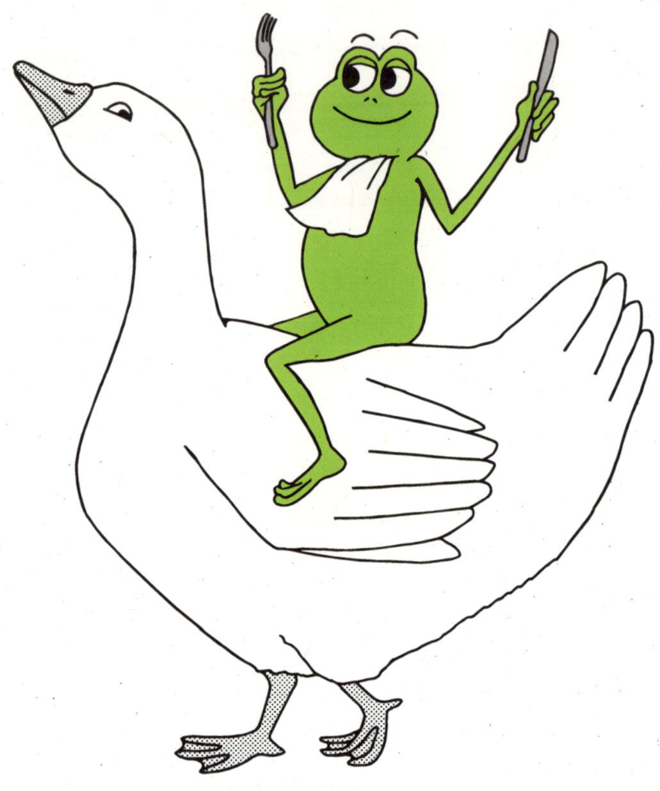

Foie Gras

A pricey preparation made from the livers of geese or ducks who are fed vast quantities of cornmeal – rather more than they'd fancy – to fatten up their most expensive organ. The rich, buttery meat may be whipped up into a mousse or *pâté*, or served *au naturel*, fried in butter with truffles or prunes.

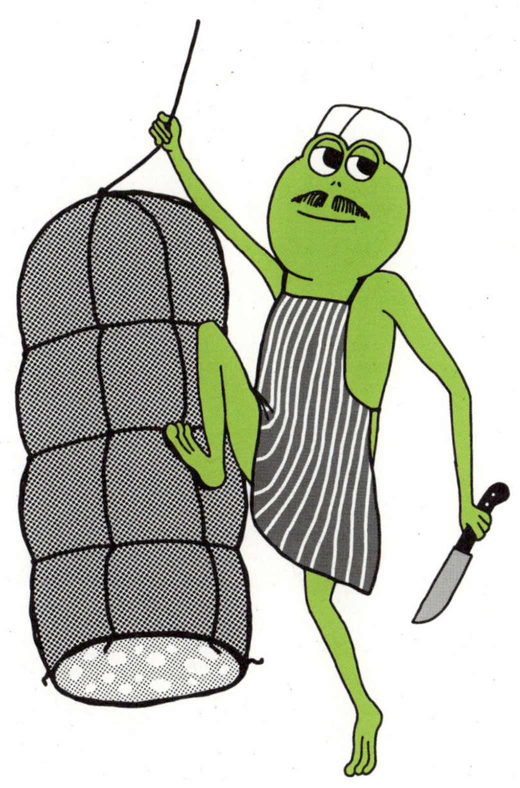

Saucisson

This salami of French pigs is a major player on the *charcuterie* board. Like the Italian variety, *Saucisson* is made predominantly from pork, though often other animals – and even their cheeses – are thrown into the mix, along with wine, herbs and garlic. You might spot one hanging in the pantry, emitting a savoury perfume.

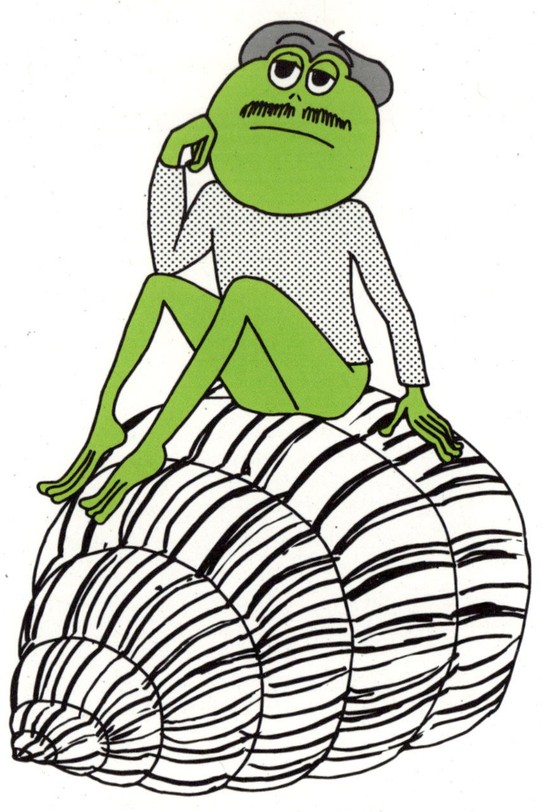

Escargots

The nuisance you know and despise from your garden, fried up with garlic and butter. Must be eaten with a surgical instrument designed especially for the task. Whilst sinking your teeth into your somewhat rubbery supper, know that the snails themselves enjoyed their own final meal of plain white flour and nothing else.

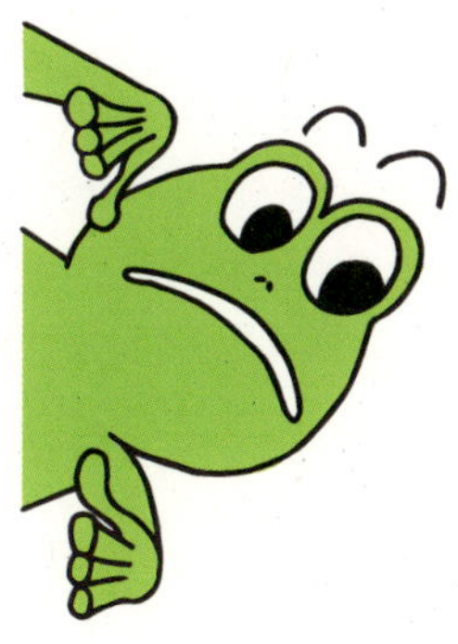

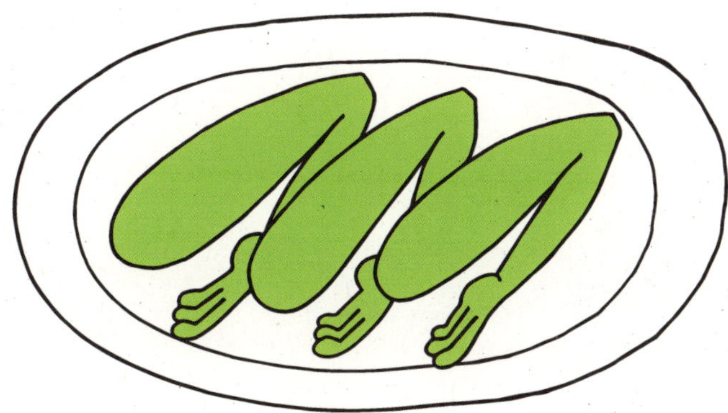

Cuisses de Grenouille

A classic French snack made by sautéing the hind-quarters of amphibians with herbs and butter. In appearance, this dish may evoke memories of small green pond-dwellers, but in flavour it's pure chicken. All in all, a meal for those precious few with a sense of adventure.

Editor's note – the nature of this dish may offend some amphibious readers.

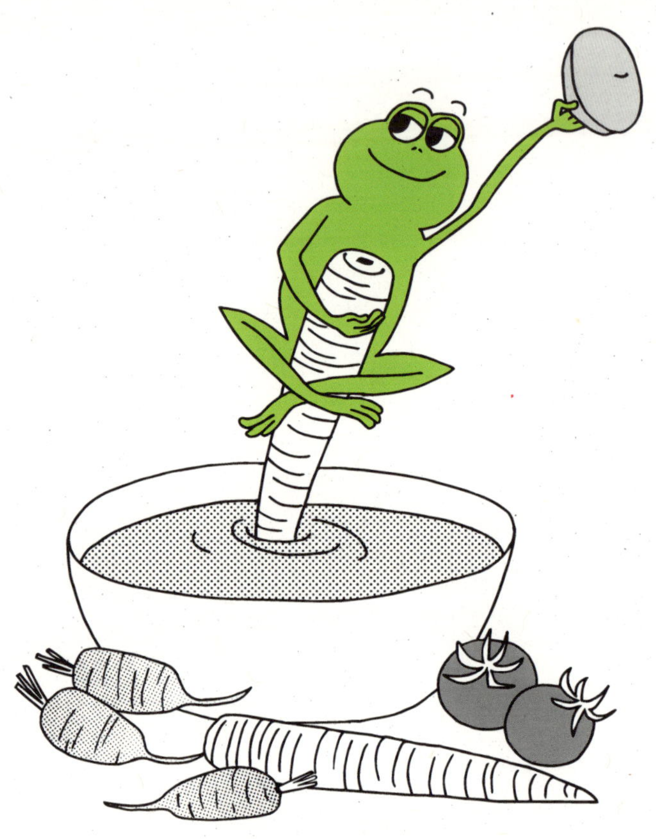

Crudités

A colourful appetizer of assorted crunchy vegetables, sliced and artfully arranged on a platter. Dipping food directly into butter and salt – perhaps a habit normally reserved for the privacy of the home – is, in this case, entirely acceptable.

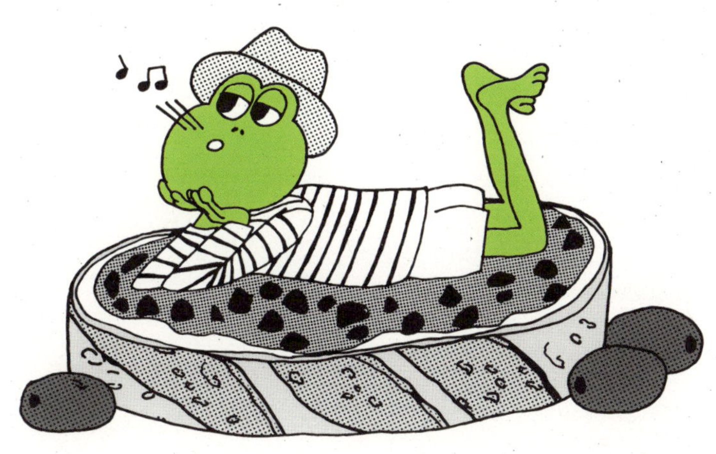

Tapenade

A black, briny preparation that brings all the salt of the Mediterranean sea to a spread. Olives, garlic, anchovies and capers are ground to a purée; ready to slather on meat, fish or crusty bread as a *pètit Provençal* accompaniment to an *apéritif*.

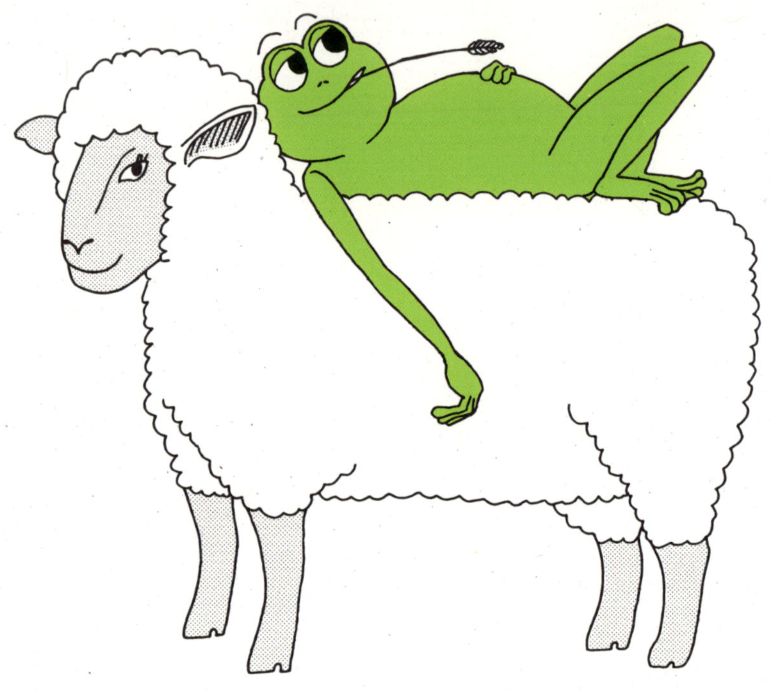

Roquefort

This star of the blue-vein cheese world originated, like us all, in a cave. Milk is gathered from stoic ewes grazing in the barren lands of the Combalou plateau, and left to ripen in limestone caves. The result is an eye-wateringly tangy *fromage*, best washed down with sweet sips of *Muscat* or white wine. May also enliven a sandwich, salad dressing or *soufflé*.

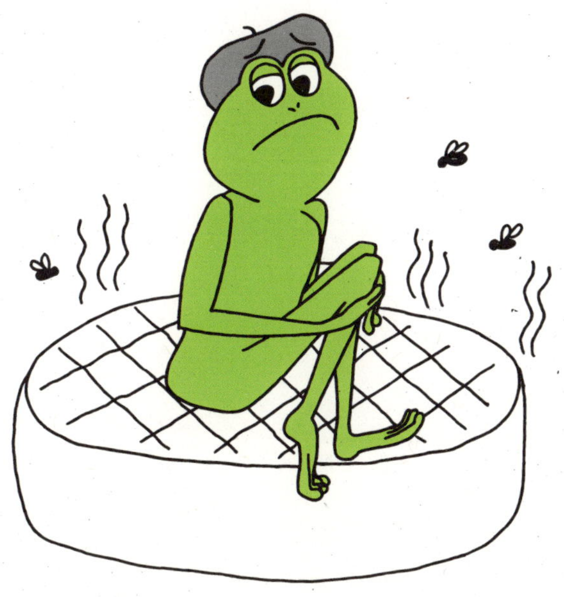

Camembert

Creamy round wheels of heaven, produced by the angelic cows of Normandy. Signature *Camembert* characteristics are a soft rind coated with white mould, and a supple yellow interior that oozes (deliciously) with age. May be baked until molten, as a party trick. *Un peu* fragrant when allowed to fully ripen. Worth it.

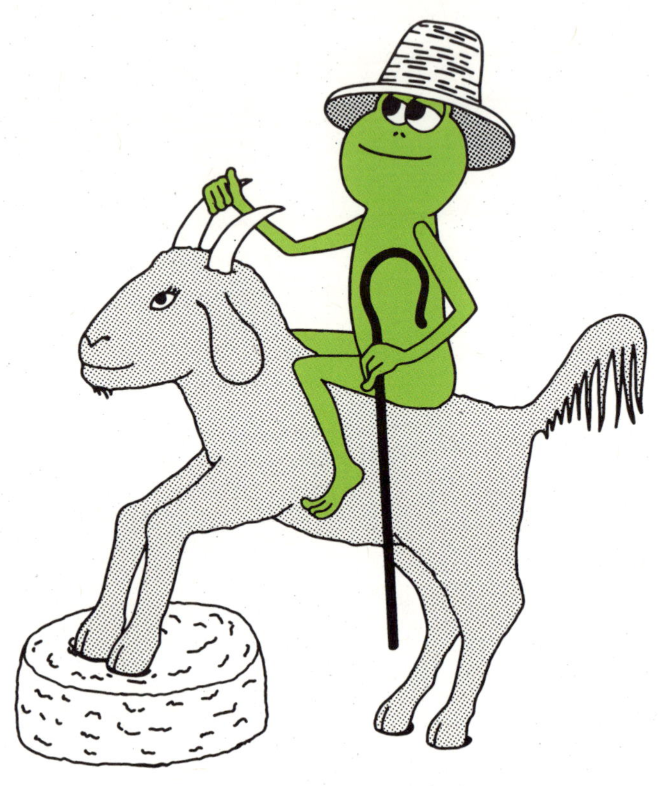

Fromage du Chèvre

Milk of the goat is formed into various geometric shapes and either consumed *très fraiche* or left to age. Look out for *roulàdes* (cylinders), *crottins* (small rounds) or *pyramides* of this fine creamy stuff, often artfully rolled in ash, herbs or spices. A salad of warm *chèvre,* soft lettuce and crunchy walnuts drizzled with honey should feature on the menu of every good French bistro.

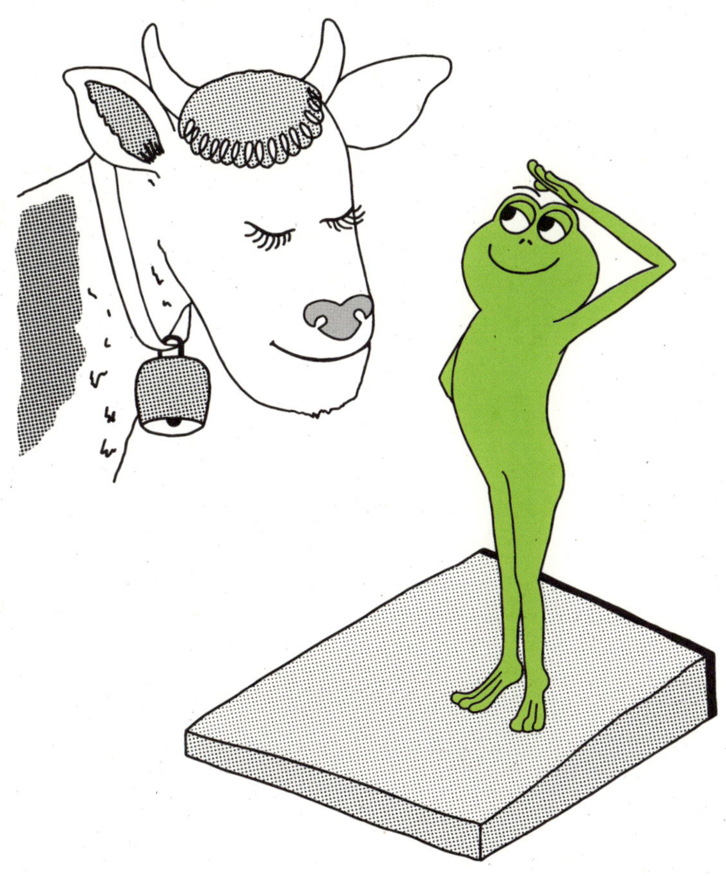

Comté

The favourite cheese of the country's 500 or so varieties, according to the people. The Jura alps provide *Comté* cows with the perfect combination of fresh air, sweeping views and green grass to produce milk that is transported down the hill and fermented for 6 to 36 months. Wheels of *Comté* come as wide as 70cm and must be sliced up according to a complex diagram.

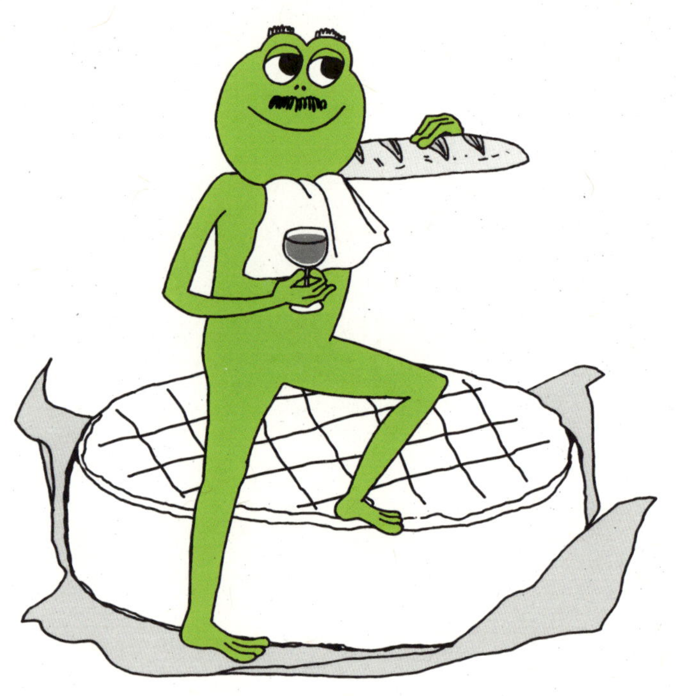

Déjeuner

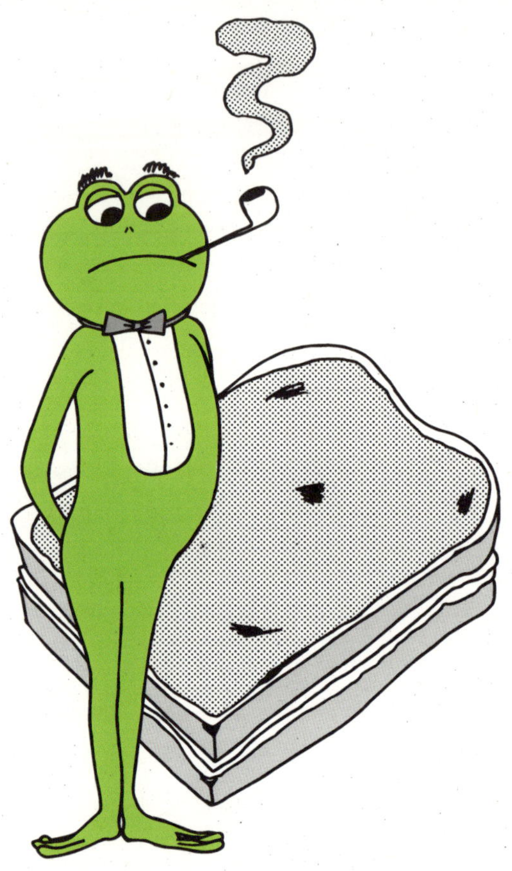

Croque Monsieur

His 'n' hers toasties. Sliced *Gruyère* cheese and ham are sandwiched between thick wodges of fluffy white *pain de mie* and pan-fried until *croquant* – crunchy – inspiring the name of this snack. A lashing of *Béchamel* may be added for a little more luxe.

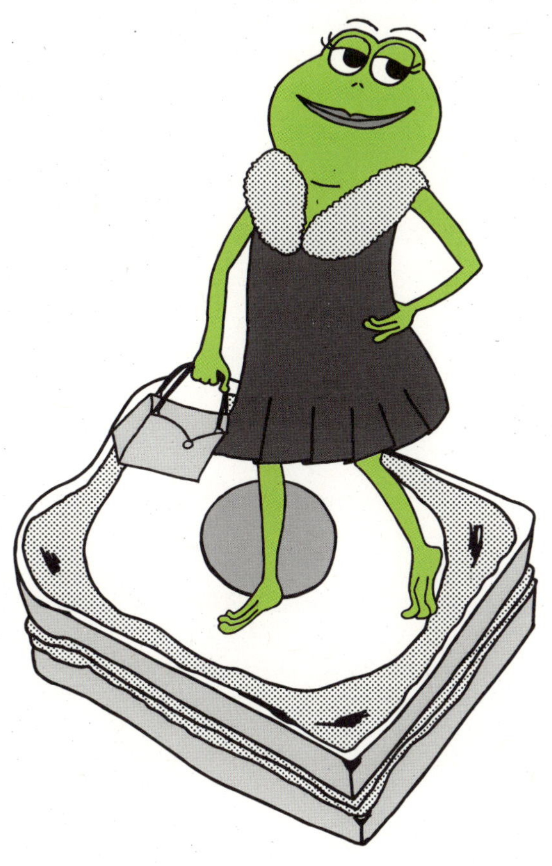

Croque Madame

Madame takes her sandwich with a fried egg on top. Their daughter, the *Croque Mademoiselle*, is a *végétarienne*, and goes entirely *sans-jambon* altogether.

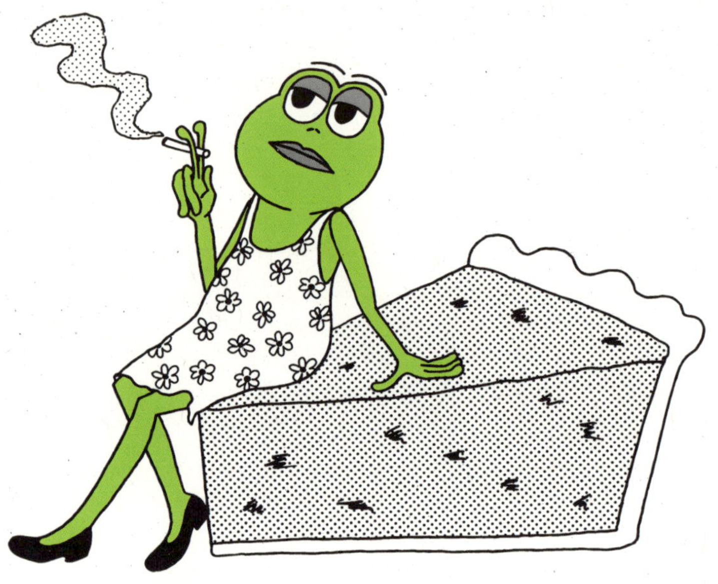

Quiche Lorraine

French for 'bacon and egg pie'. This tarted up *version Française* sees a mixture of whipped eggs, cream and *lardons* enrobed in a buttery pastry crust and baked 'til light and fluffy. May be served hot or cold. Very yummy.

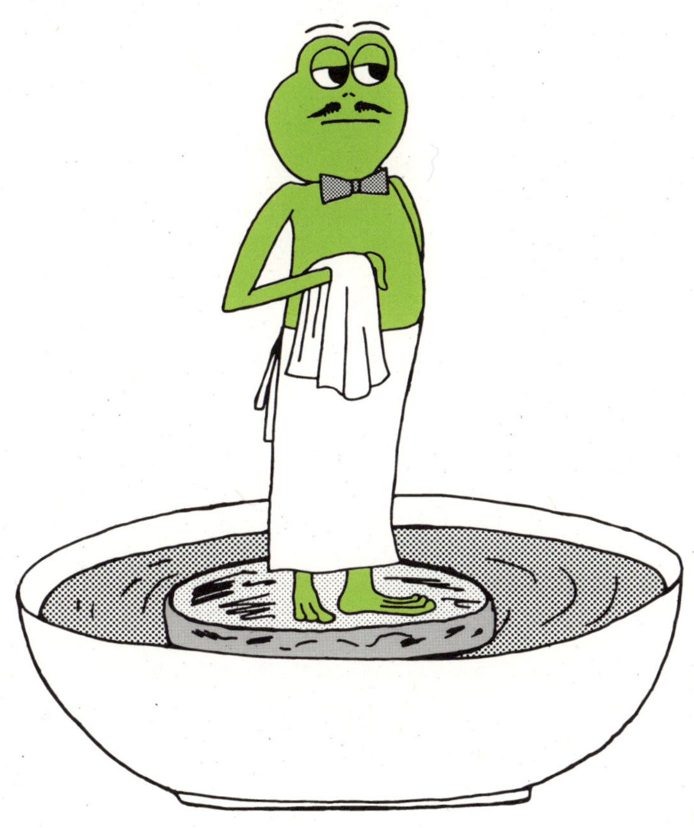

Soupe a L'Oignon

A soup that's rather emotional to prepare, and again to digest. Hundreds of onions are sacrificed in the kitchen and sautéed for hours with a little wine and a lot of butter, until sweet. Served with a floating island of *baguette* topped with melted cheese.

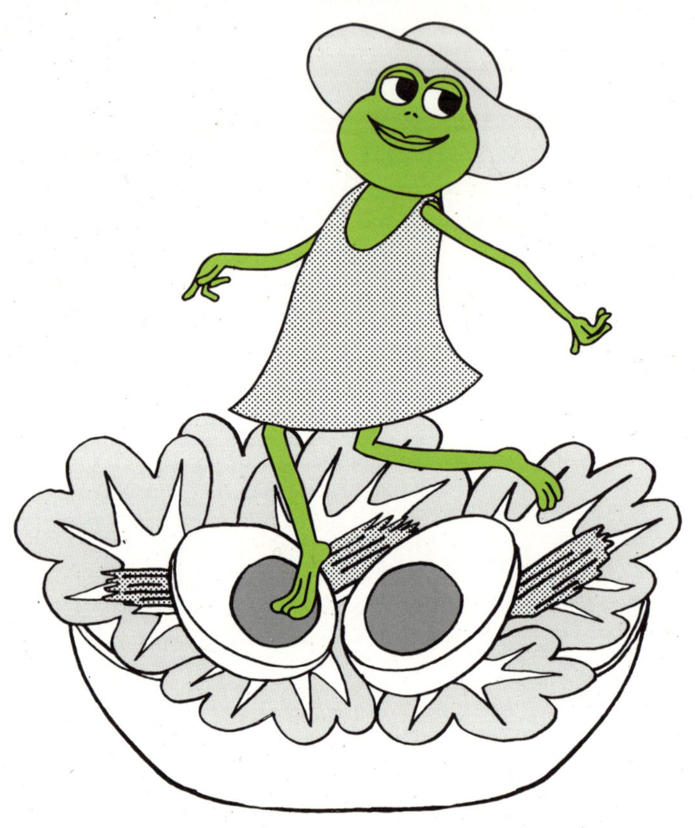

Salade Niçoise

Just what the doctor ordered after a hard day on the Côte d'Azur in the sun. A green salad with boiled eggs and potatoes is jazzed up with such Mediterranean touches as black olives, tomatoes, anchovies and tuna – though unlikely from today's catch.

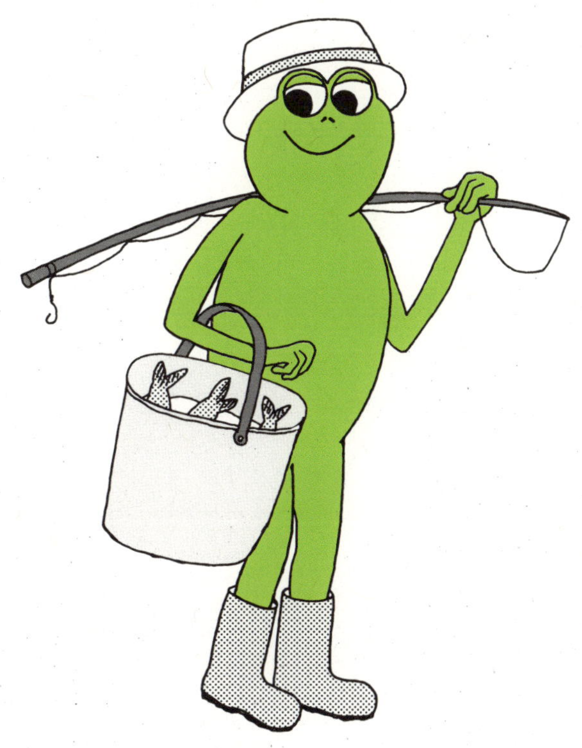

Pissaladière

This *Provençal* pizza is topped with a truckload of caramelised onions and garnished with a lattice of anchovies. Extra seasoning comes from thyme, black olives and the tears of the poor chef who made it. A truly delicious southern snack.

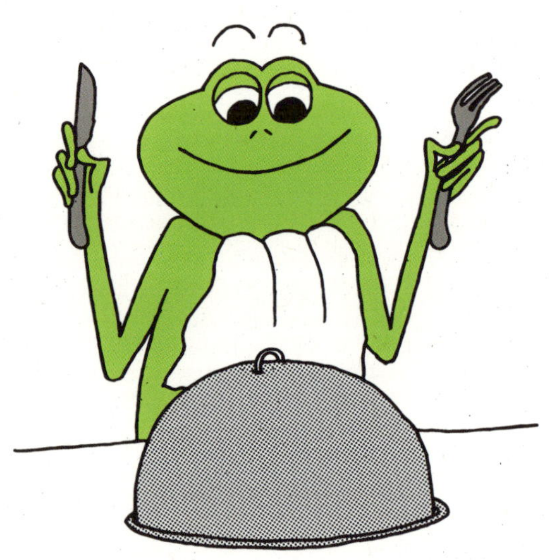

Plats

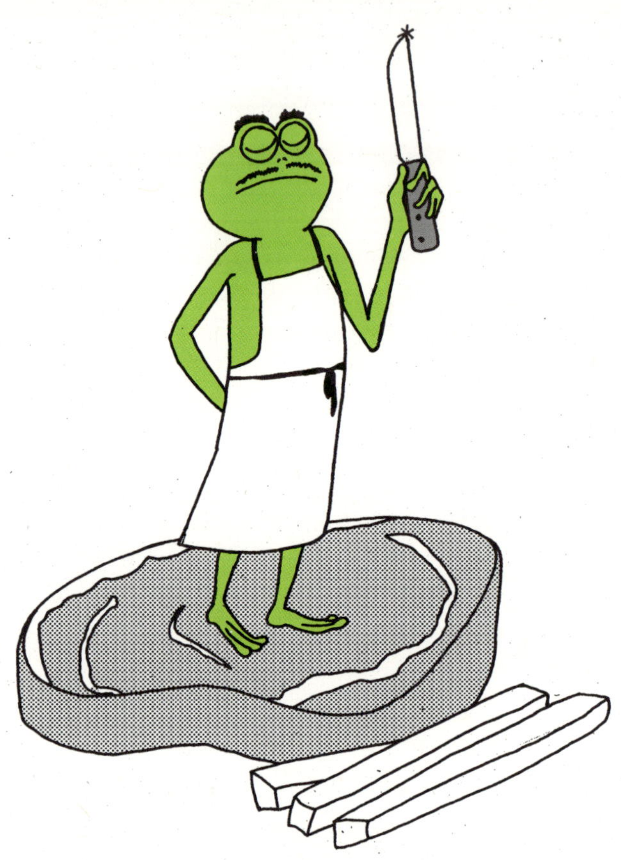

Steak Frîtes

A cut of cow served with everyone's favourite deep-fried potatoes, sliced *à la Julienne* – twice as thick as matches. It's quite acceptable to request your steak cooked blue and bloody. Popular adornments include garlic butter, pepper sauce, *Béarnaise* sauce or Dijon mustard. A leaf or two of *salade* may grace the plate, for colour.

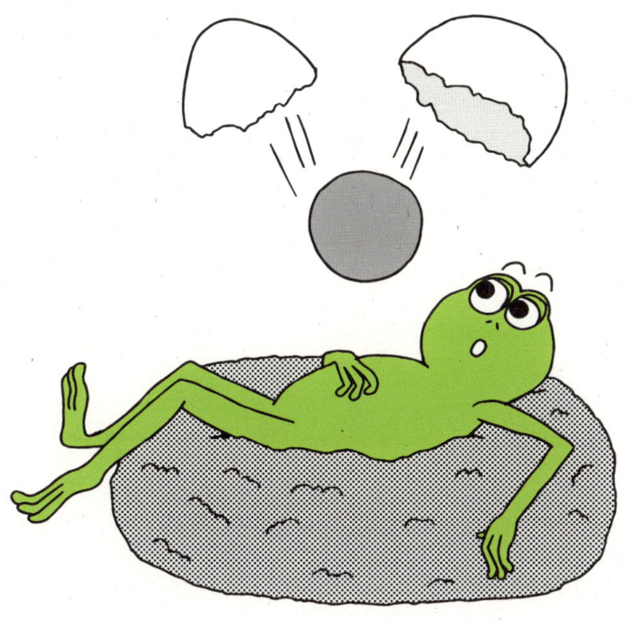

Tartare de Bœuf

This steak does not come medium, well-done or even 'done' at all. Beef is minced, raw, then served with freshly cracked pepper and a freshly cracked egg – also raw. May be topped with a few crisps. May put hair on your chest.

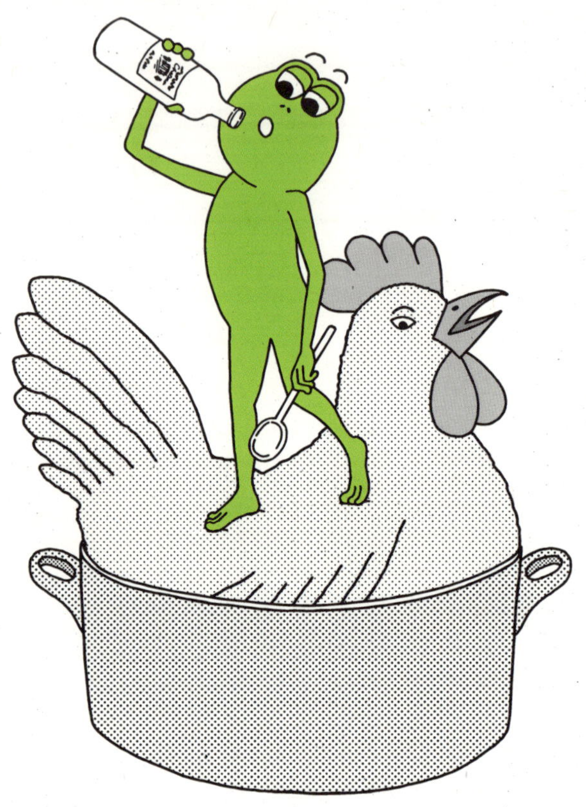

Coq au Vin

A drunken chicken is laid to rest in France's finest grape juice amongst a couple of onions and mushrooms. While this dish was designed to soften a tough old rooster, a younger, less vocal chook is advised for best results.

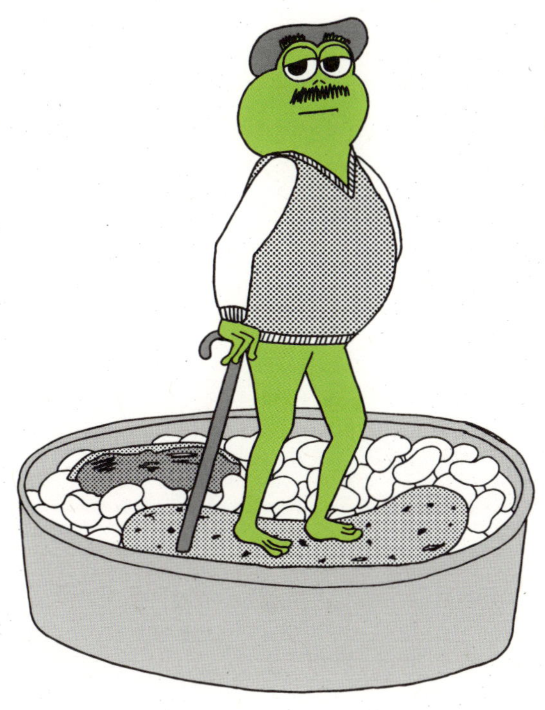

Cassoulet

A terracotta crock-pot of mysterious slow-cooked meats floating in a stodgy sea of garlicky white *haricot* beans. Despite a total lack of greens, you will be rewarded with any combination of Toulouse sausage, pork, goose, duck, lamb and perhaps a few bits of mutton too.

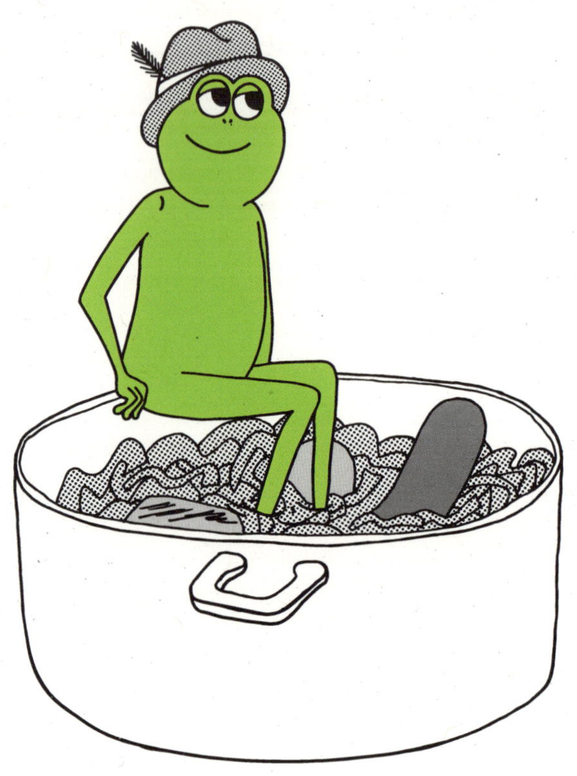

Choucroute Garnie

A rustic preparation of pickled cabbage cooked in white wine, inspired by Germany over the hill. Amongst the *sauerkraut* you'll find boiled potatoes, various pieces of smoked pork and a *Frankfurter* (or similar) sausage. The ideal fortification for a day's hiking or hunting in the alps. A fancied-up version, *Choucroute Royale* calls for the cabbage to be cooked in Champagne.

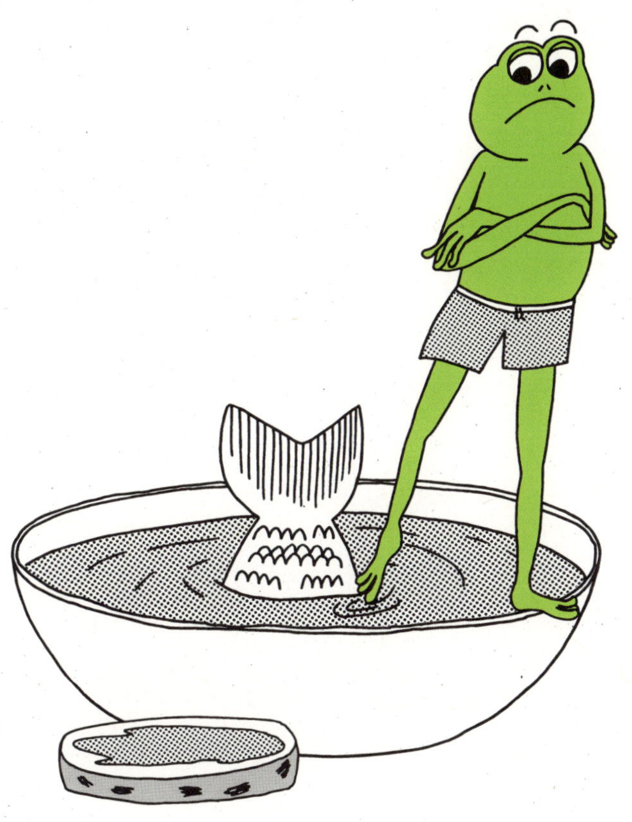

Bouillabaisse

A chalky soup of mysterious fishy ingredients enriched with tomatoes, garlic, fennel and pricey golden threads of saffron. The particular selection of *fruits de mer* varies with each day's catch. The dish is served with little rounds of toasted bread slathered with garlic-infused *Rouille* mayonnaise and a sprinkling of *fromage*. Delicious, even if *un peu* on the nose.

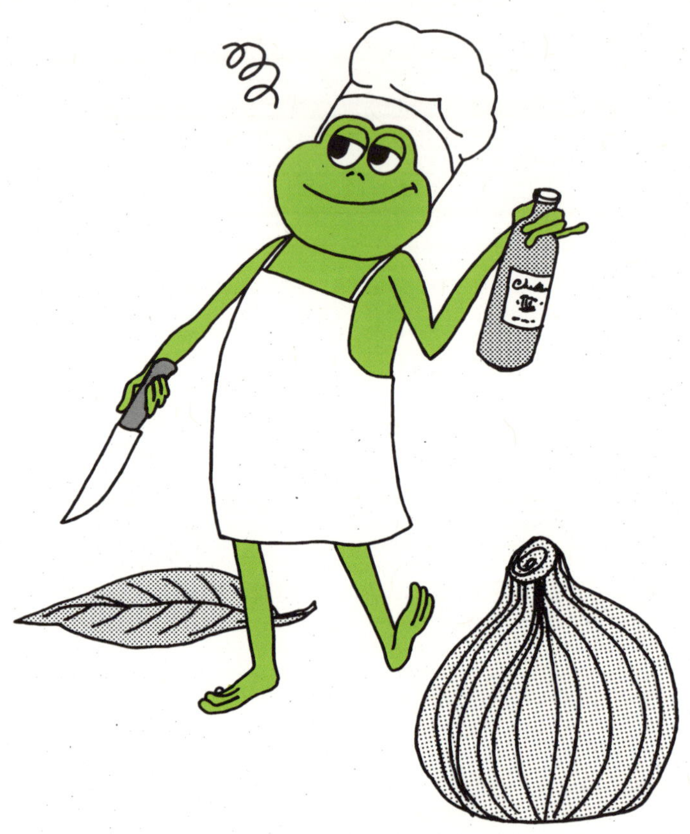

Bœuf Bourguignon

A hearty casserole of beef drowned in red wine from Burgundy with a couple of carrots, onions and mushrooms thrown in the pot for good measure. Serve alongside a glass of the same stuff you cooked with.

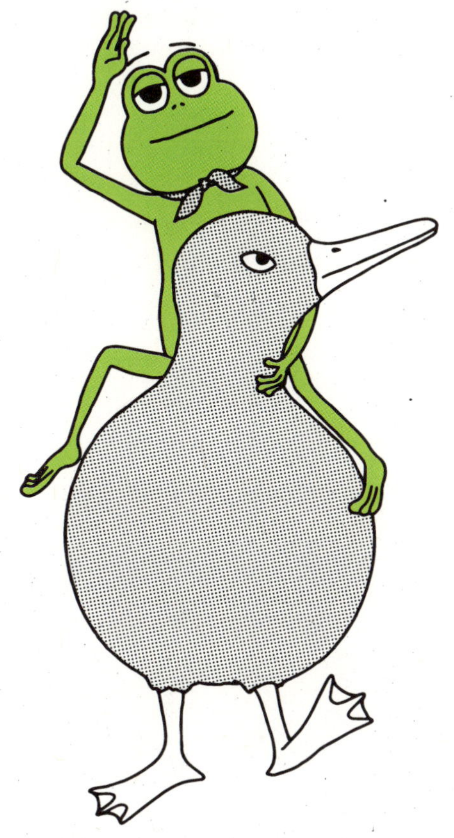

Confit de Canard

Flesh of the duck is salted and slow-cooked in its own fat with garlic and herbs. It is then stuffed into jars and stored for months ... or years. To serve, empty out the contents of the jar and fry it all up with a few potatoes. Round out the meal with a green salad on the side.

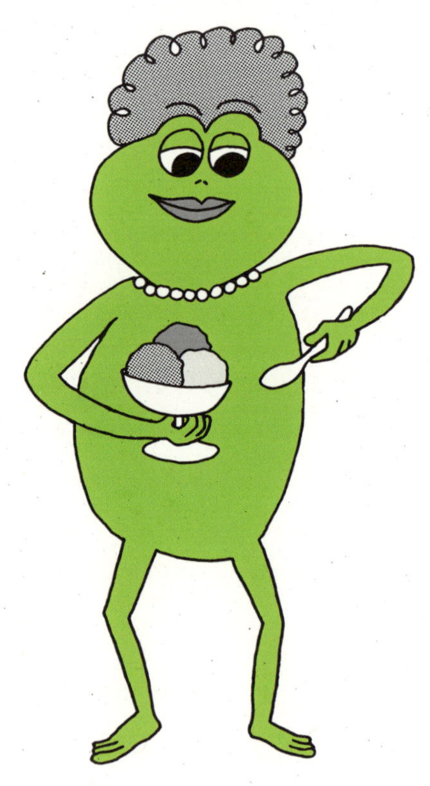

Desserts

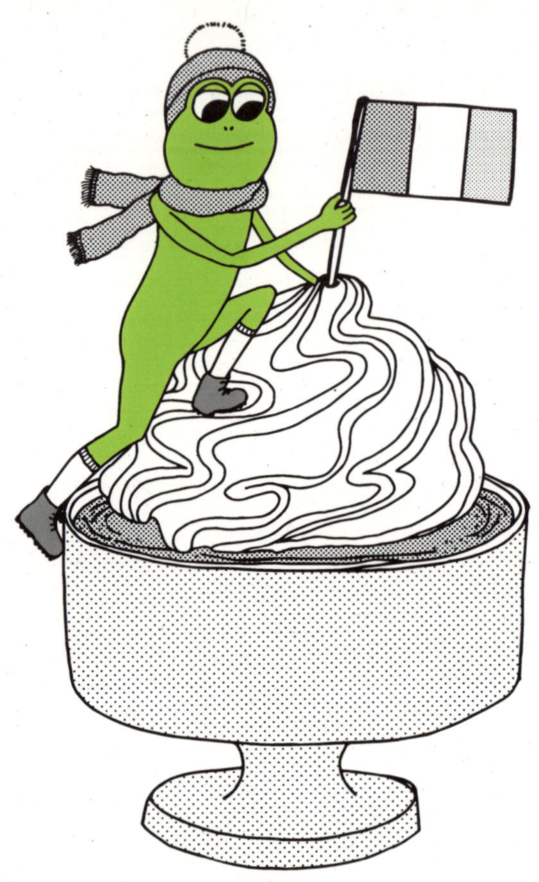

Mont Blanc

A towering slope of luxurious *crème de marrons* (chestnut purée), piled high with whipped *Chantilly* cream. Best climbed slowly so as to avoid indigestion – but watch your footing, the slippery summit has seen many casualties.

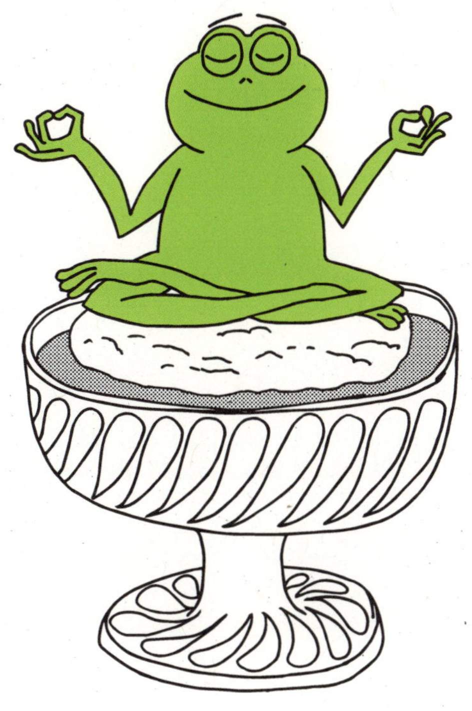

Île Flottante

Next time you're requested to visualise a peaceful, calming island for the purpose of meditation, this is your place. A featherlight poached *meringue* silently floats in a sea of vanilla *crème Anglaise*, awaiting its gentle devouring. Zen and delicious.

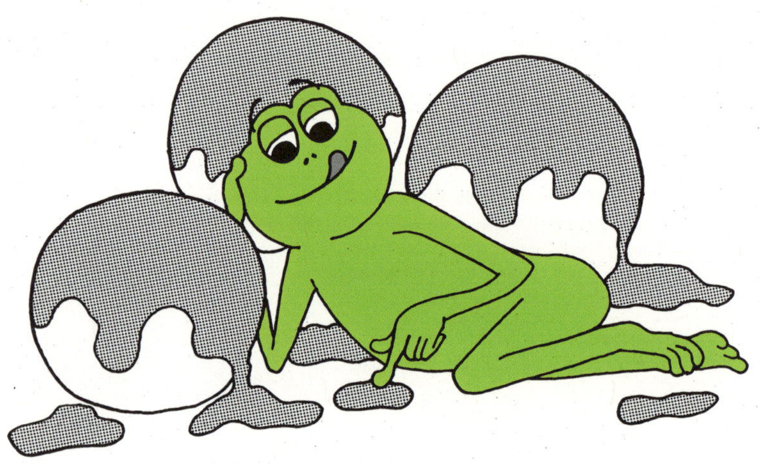

Profiteroles

A little collection of *choux* pastry puffs are filled with either *Chantilly* cream, *pâtisserie* cream or vanilla ice-cream then arranged on a plate and doused with chocolate *gânache*. A sprinkling of *praline* nuts might add additional garnish, and crunch. This may not be the most adventurous of French desserts, but it has plenty of that *je ne sais quoi* none-the-less.

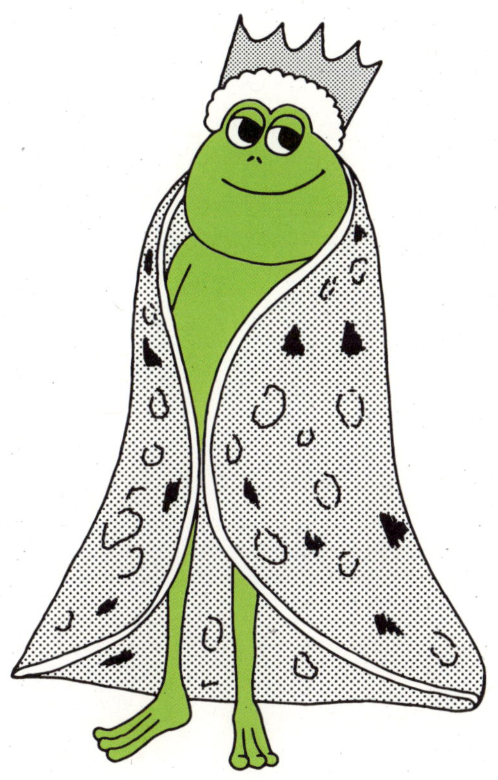

Crêpes

The larger, flatter, *Frenchier* answer to a pancake. Cooked on a griddle with a special tool for spreading by expert street vendors and *mamies* alike. Serve with jam, Nutella or a sprinkling of sugar and a spritz of lemon; syrup and bacon are never on the menu. For an additional touch of theatre, douse the fry-pan generously with Grand Marnier and light on fire to make *Crêpes Suzette*.

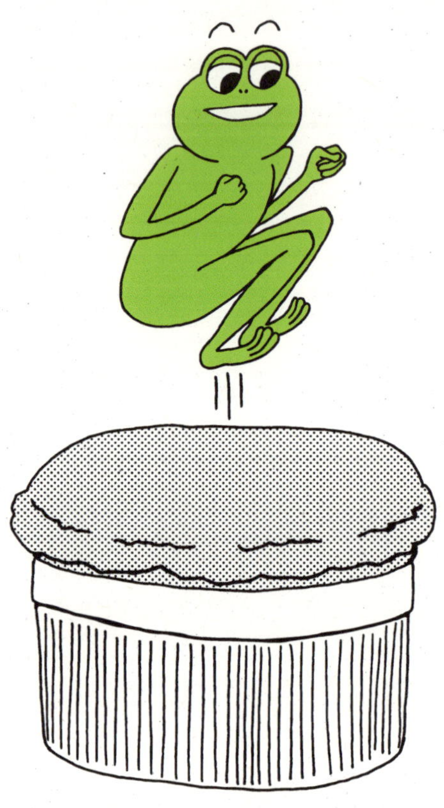

Soufflé

A sweet or savoury affair, crafted from eggs and a whole lot of hot air in the kitchen. When successful, the featherlight *soufflé* will stand proudly puffed, as its name declares, but for how long, nobody can say. If you catch wind of the *soufflé* being near-ready, proceed *à la table* immediately, before it collapses ... or the chef does.

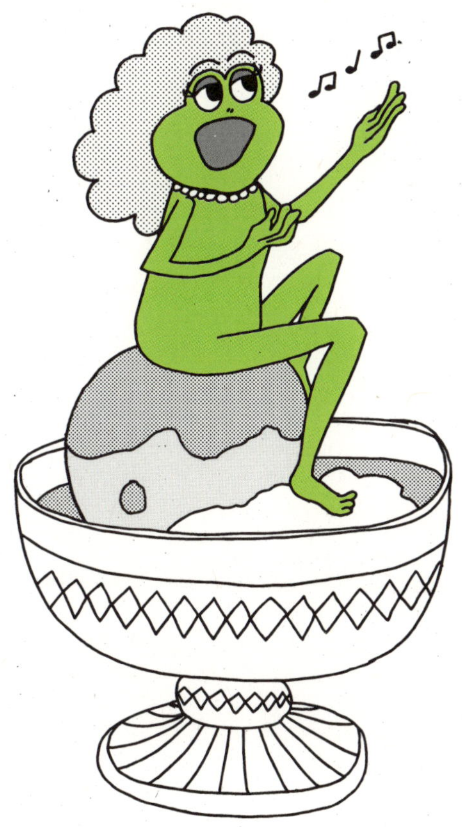

Pêche Melba

A dessert as strong and well-rounded as an opera singer's voice. Vanilla ice-cream is paired with half a poached peach, bathed in raspberry *coulis*, then garnished with whipped *Chantilly* cream. Hits all the high notes.

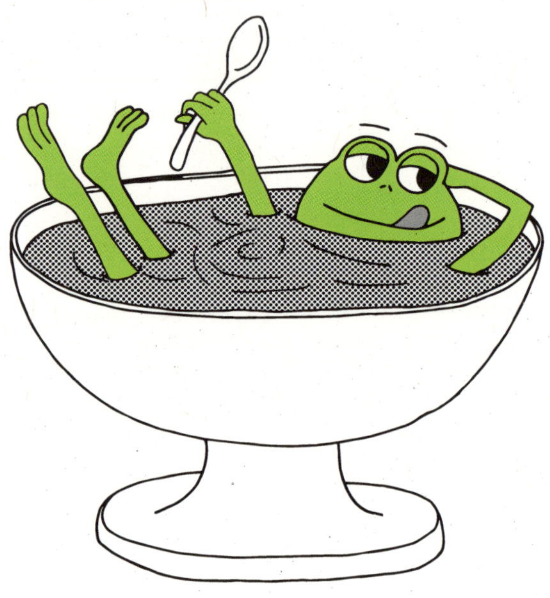

Mousse au Chocolat

As if by magic, chocolate is made to appear as light as a cloud with the incorporation of air. In fact it is rendered all the heavier thanks to the addition of eggs, sugar, cream, butter or all of the above. Possibly one of the most delicious things on earth.

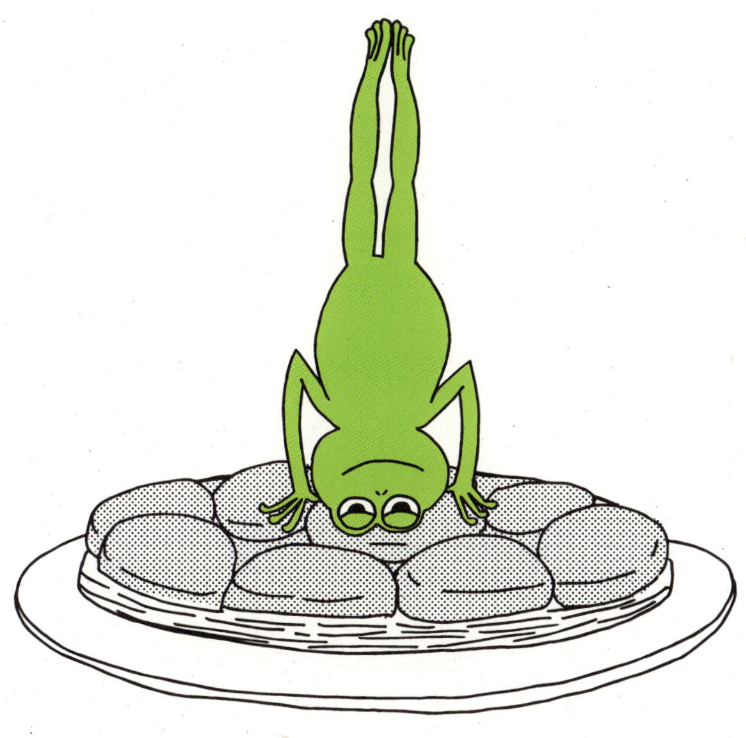

Tarte Tatin

A topsy-turvy treatment of pastry with apples caramelised in butter and sugar. It was created, legend has it, entirely by accident by two sisters on the outskirts of Paris. When righted, this reverse cake is entirely delicious.

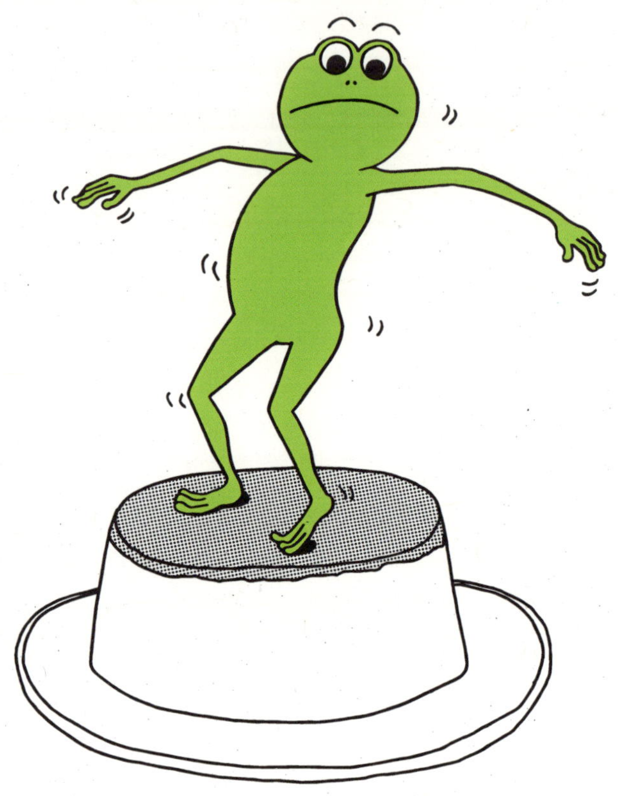

Crème Caramel

A divine fate for eggs, baked and set under a melting lid of oozing burnt caramel. Cooked upside down in a *bain-marie* and reversed to serve, this is custard with a French twist.

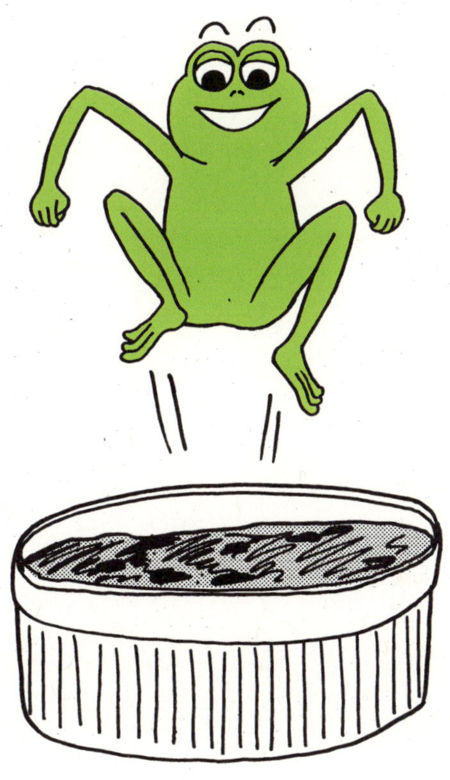

Crème Brûlée

This dessert likely inspired the expression *la crème de la crème* – sweets don't get much better. Fresh cream is enriched with eggs, perfumed with vanilla and gently baked in a water bath. A toasted sugar crust is added before serving; requiring a brief outburst of violence to crack open the dessert, and nothing but gentle murmurs of delight thereafter.

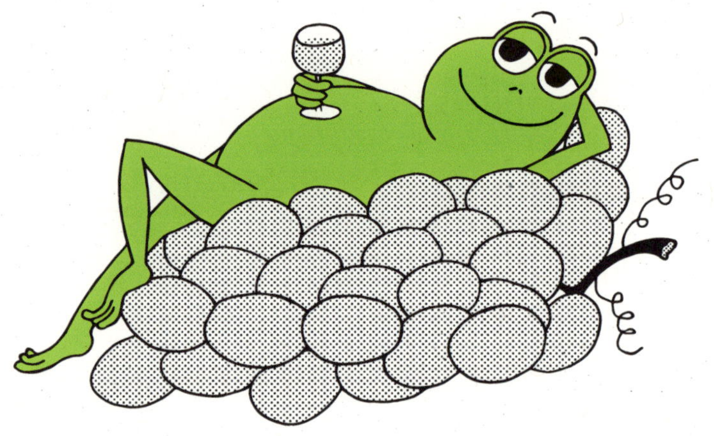

Boissons

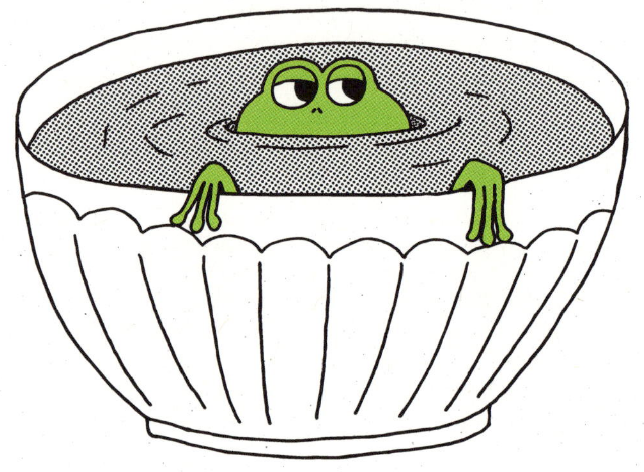

Café au Lait

A large warm bowl in which the French bathe each morning. Acceptable transportation vehicles for coffee to-mouth include *croissants*, lumps of *brioche* and *tartines* – slices of day-old *baguette* slathered with butter and jam.

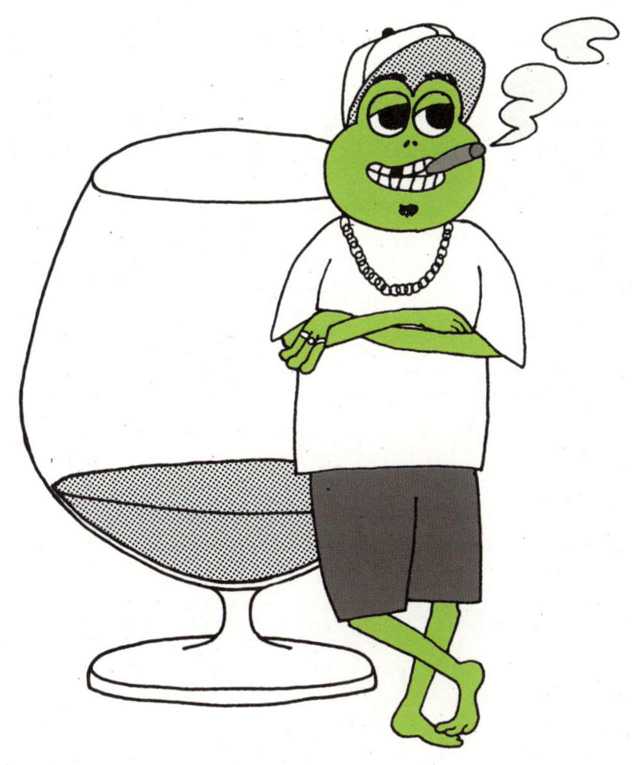

Cognac

An expensive golden liquid, routinely splashed around by rappers as a display of one's riches. This eponymous brandy from the commune of Cognac is aged in oak barrels for decades, growing darker as the years go by. The real top-shelf stuff earns the right to a pure crystal bottle. Must be consumed from giant balloon-shaped glasses.

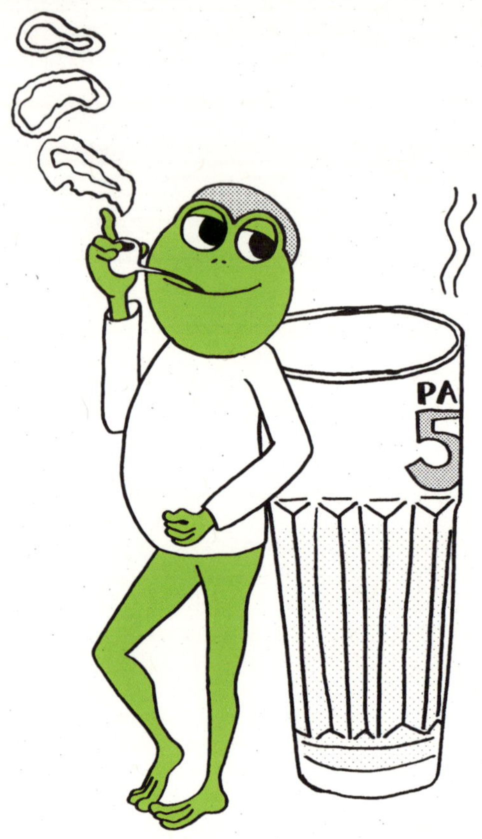

Pastis

A powerful aniseed beverage that's something of an acquired taste. Magically turns from clear to cloudy when topped up with water. Pastis is best enjoyed by the sea down south with a game of *pétanque*. May help you locate an appetite before a meal, then digest the meal afterwards. Locals will affirm that the *real* Pastis is made in Marseille.

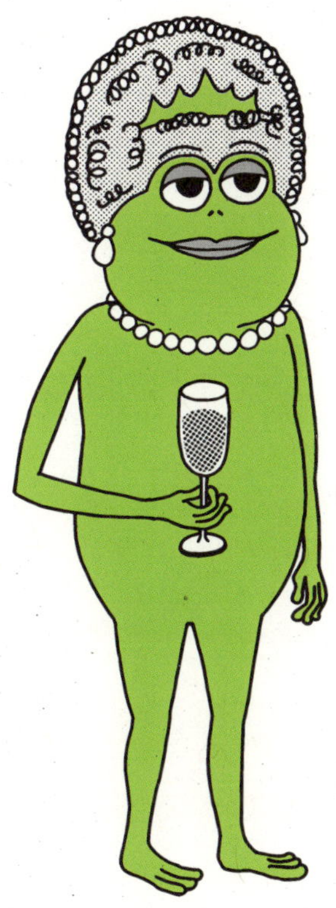

Kir Royale

A chic elevation of Champagne, coloured purple by the addition of *Crème de Cassis* – the alcoholic *jus* of blackcurrants. Perhaps France's finest cocktail *apéritif*. Best consumed while wearing a Chanel twinset and pearls. *Chin chin!*

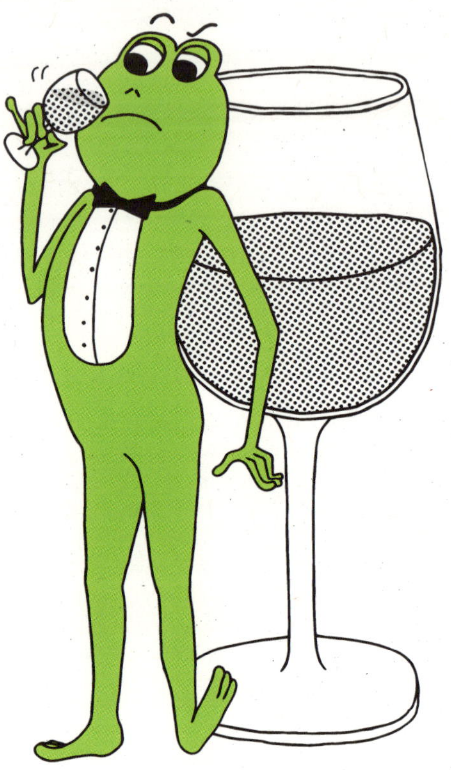

Vin

Eh oui, wine runs in the blood of all Frenchmen – topped up twice daily, as per doctor's orders, at lunch and dinner. Option for a third infusion at breakfast if desired. Whether *rouge, blanc* or *rosé* in colour, all wine is made by fermenting grapes with a whole lot of hoopla. Wax lyrical about vintage, *terroir* and tasting notes at the table if you wish to sound sophisticated.

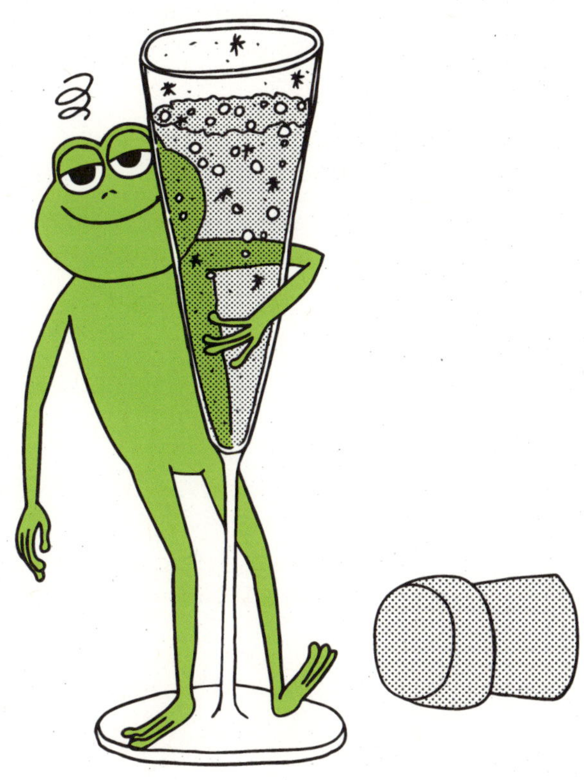

Champagne

Once the exclusive beverage of French royalty, *Champers* has trickled down to become a favourite of the people. This fizzy wine is the world-standard for celebrating everything from the end of the work day to marriages and milestone birthdays. Despite its reputation as a feminine drop, it's perfectly acceptable for the *monsieurs* to spray hundreds of euros worth of it over a crowd after winning a car race. Watch out for the cork to the eye.

FRENCH CUISINE – *A Frog's Guide*

Conceived and created in the prune-growing region of Southwest France, with the help of a few frogs.

First published in 2022 by Carte Blanche in an edition of 400.

ISBN: 978-0-646-87110-3

www.aliceoehr.com